What Others
Are Saying

Cochise helps us with common misunderstandings of dog behavior such as begging, eating trash, and dog food.

—Animal Radio

This book is the perfect gift for every human-dog family. It is full of humorous truths about who trains whom.

—About-Books

the Puppies' Guide to Training Humans

the Puppies' Guide to Training Humans

All We Need is Unconditional Love

By Cochise & Keith Barksdale

TATE PUBLISHING & Enterprises

Published by Tate Publishing & Enterprises, LLC
127 E. Trade Center Terrace | Mustang, Oklahoma 73064 USA
1.888.361.9473 | www.tatepublishing.com

Tate Publishing is committed to excellence in the publishing industry. The company reflects the philosophy established by the founders, based on Psalm 68:11,
"The Lord gave the word and great was the company of those who published it."

Book design copyright © 2009 by Tate Publishing, LLC. All rights reserved.
Cover design by Cole Roberts
Interior design by Jeff Fisher

Published in the United States of America

ISBN: 978-1-61566-134-3
Pets, Dogs, Training
09.10.09

The Puppies' Guide to Training Humans

All We Need Is Unconditional Love

Cochise Barksdale

With typing assistance from Human
Companion Keith Barksdale

Dedication

This book is dedicated to late author Cochise Barksdale, who brought an amazing amount of love into my life. It is also dedicated to Sequoia, Lulu, Grizzly, Buddy, Lilly, Gabe, and all those puppies that live in our hearts and shape our behavior with unconditional love.

Table of Contents

Preface

This is a book written by a dog. It is a training guide for dogs that has been known among the dog community worldwide for many years. Most humans will assume this is a dog-training manual in the usual sense, but it is just the opposite. It is the truth behind who trains whom. *Sniff, sniff, lick, lick.* As any dog owner, or *human companion,* as we prefer to call them, will begrudgingly admit, dogs train people!

Comedian Jerry Seinfeld once said something to the effect that if he visited Earth from another planet, he would think dogs were the ruling species. After all, where else would one observe humans following dogs around and picking up their poop?

In this guide we will share training techniques and explore from a dog's viewpoint the absurd but accepted human views of dogs. Take dog treats for example: Why are they called *treats?* Sure, we sit and roll over when offered a bone-shaped thing with the texture of stale bread, but they are not really treats. We are just happy to have anything other than dog food. If humans ate the same food every day, every meal, they'd salivate over an earthworm just for the change. Does that make it a *treat?*

At the age of four weeks, I (Cochise) was placed in a home for unwanted pets with my brothers and sisters. Because of this place, I was able to obtain a good human companion and enjoy a long and comfortable dog life. Thus, I will be donating a portion of the profits from this book to various dog-supporting organizations for the continued support of homeless dogs in the hope that they also find suitable homes.

—Love without borders or conditions,
Cochise

Author Cochise Barksdale at his New York home, enjoying the comforts of his sofa.

Special note from Adam and Eve Barksdale

This book was written almost entirely by Cochise but was not completed when he went to doggie heaven. We never had the honor of meeting Cochise, but through studying and being influenced by his writings, we came to love and admire him. He was a special dog, uniquely able to capture the nature of dogs around the world. Our role was a humble one; we assembled Cochise's notes, pictures, and other documentation. Cochise's loving human companion, Keith, was very helpful in providing the necessary support to help get this book to print. As a memorial to Cochise, it is dedicated to every dog. It was Cochise's hope that all breeds from all walks of life have the best of what dog life has to offer them.

A Note from Keith Barksdale

Cochise and I were companions for fourteen years. In his last few years he lost his eyesight as the result of an operation to remove a tumor. He never stopped giving love, and he taught me a lot about this emotion. He holds a special place in my heart. Like humans I have become close with, he will always be inside me even though he is no longer physically present.

I could not simply bury Cochise, so when he passed I had him cremated. His ashes, his collar, and his two favorite squeaky toys are in a container that maintains a position of honor and remembrance next to my bed.

After Cochise passed away, I wondered about inviting another puppy into my life. Then I remembered the joy Cochise had brought me. So began my search for another puppy.

A friend of mine had mentioned a street

litter in an abandoned building at a parking lot in town. When I arrived, the parking attendant told me about the litter of puppies. He had been feeding and taking care of them. They were the offspring of the dog that hung around the parking lot. He took me to see the litter. I peeked inside the building to view what seemed to be a herd of puppies. It was the largest litter I had ever seen— more than a dozen little piggy puppies waddling around broken cement doing what puppies do: exploring, eating, and sleeping. One of the puppies was immediately at my feet checking me out, as if acting as the inspector for the group. She and I played for a while. The others either watched or ignored us.

Then my eye caught sight of another puppy hiding behind a plank of wood. He was off by himself, kind of an outcast, runt of the litter. He was watching me, obviously scared. In addition to being the runt and outcast, he also had a much different color from the rest. The majority of the puppies in the litter were black with brown accents, like rottweilers. This guy behind the plank was beige and blond, more like a light brown doberman. He was hiding and silent, but I was

Cochise Barksdale

drawn to him. I went over to him, and he looked at me and in an instant communicated trust, love, sadness, and hope from his hazel-brown eyes. I could not leave him there. This was Adam.

As I picked Adam up, the group inspector trotted toward me and sat on my right foot, looking up at me and her brother. This was Eve. I realized that I was not leaving with one puppy; I was being blessed by the companionship of a brother and sister. I picked up Eve; at the time they both could be carried in one arm and looked like hamsters. The three of us said goodbye to the other puppies, Adam and Eve's brothers and sisters. The parking attendant charged me five dollars for my two new puppy companions and off we went, home. I returned occasionally to drop off bags of puppy food for the parking attendant and to see a few of Adam and Eve's brothers and sisters, but eventually, after a few weeks, they were all adopted.

I decided to publish Cochise's manuscript to help other dogs with their human companions and humans with their search for unconditional love.

Eve, Keith, and Adam Barksdale (left to right)

People—Picking the Right One

As puppies, one of the first things we need to do is to find a companion. It seems to me that we have three paths. One is to be born into a family where the humans decide to keep you. The other is where the humans decide to share the wonderful puppies they have with others. The third is when, for whatever reason, we are born and placed in an adoption center. In the first instance we have nothing to worry about; in the other two paths we need to be prepared to attract and pick humans we like. So this chapter is to help puppies understand more about humans and share favorable and unfavorable characteristics to look for as well as how to attract and select the human of your choice.

Humans use the terms *master* or *owner* to designate their role with a puppy. This goes back to an ego-stroking need to declare themselves more dominant. Unfortunately, these subservient titles imply *slave* or *property,* respectively. Puppies are neither! We are companions for humans, who are companions for us. I like to call them human companions and suggest they call us puppy companions or puppy buddies. Isn't that much nicer?

Picking the right human as your companion is a delicate process. A dog must act quickly with a candidate but not make a hasty choice. Primarily, dogs have to be sure the candidate is responsible. Humans should provide care, comfort, love, and squeaky toys!

Many placement agencies provide assistance with screening. Before I selected my human companion, he had to fill out an application detailing both personal and financial information. He even signed an agreement to have me tutored. (Or at least that's what I thought. Later I found out it was not tutored but *neutered!* Ouch! Talk about a miscommunication!)

"Neutered! I thought he said tutored!"

I have three brothers and two sisters. We were orphaned and placed in a home for puppies, dogs, kittens, and cats without human companions, called the Humane Society. At the Humane Society, my siblings and I were placed in a fenced area to be on display for humans to adopt us. I'm not really knocking the place; after all, it was better at our young age than resorting to our ancestral roots and hunting for food. Can you imagine? No thanks; that is too much work—and messy work at that! I rather like the domesticated position we have aspired to over centuries of evolution.

We were treated quite well. We received food and water, we played games with the attendants, and we had the company of adult dogs and other puppies.

On the occasion that our gate would open and a prospect would come in to play with us, we had our strategy ready. We held a well-planned, *be cute* free-for-all. It went like this: When people came in, we would jump and yip, lick their fingers, bite their shoelaces, roll over on our backs to be scratched, jump up on their legs, or perform any maneuver the humans would think was cute.

A good example of a bored look

A good example of a cute look

The Puppies' Guide to Training Humans

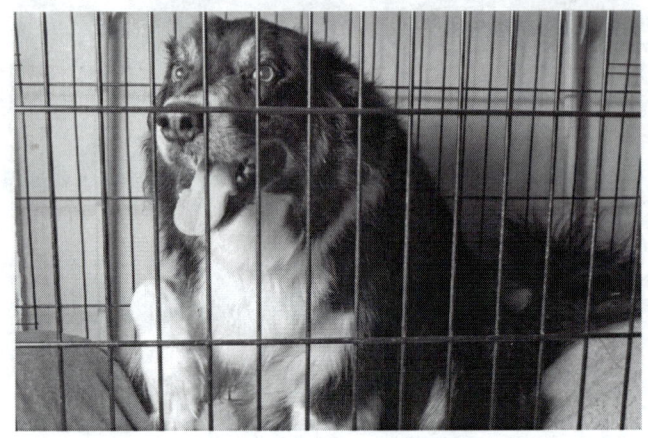

Good example of an excited happy dance

The golden rule was not to get too excited, as sometimes puppies do, and go "wee." Occasionally one of us would get out of our cage and entertain everyone by prancing down the hallway as the attendant chased us. *Sniff, sniff, lick, lick, woof!*

One by one, my brothers and sisters were adopted and carried to their new homes by their human companions. Those of us remaining wished them good luck, since it was unlikely we would ever see each other again.

After a few weeks, all my brothers and sisters had gone to good homes. And there I remained, mixed in with a few other dogs from other families. I admit I was a high-strung pup. I guess I was too hyperactive for most of the prospects.

One day the attendants came down the hall with several people and some odd-looking equipment. I knew the strange contingent gathered outside my cage were not prospects. As they set up their devices I remember thinking, *Uh oh, has my welcome run out? I am only ten and a half weeks old. My whole life is in front of me. I am not going down without a fight.* I did my best *I'm-a-little-cutie* dance; I pawed the gate and licked every finger that came near. With my squeaky puppy voice I yipped for everyone's attention.

I remember the gate opening and someone reaching in to pick me up. I saw a bright light and heard a loud clap, then silence, except for a distant, deep and serious voice saying, "Approximately nine million animals are euthanized annually in the United States. The average age of a dog in a shelter is eight months. There are thirty million puppies and kittens born every year, and approximately 43 percent of puppy births are unplanned. Only 25 percent of dogs placed in shelters are adopted. If you can help give a home to a homeless pet, please contact us."

Then my attendant handed me over to the person who was talking. I licked his finger and continued my *playful-and-cute* routine. There was more talking, and then the light faded. I looked around. The strangers passed me around from one to another. I was being praised, petted, and played with. One of them even had a treat for me to eat!

Heck, I had filmed a commercial! I had just made my TV debut! I was a television personality! I was the king of cute, the camera's canine, an activist for action! All this attention, and I could not remember the last time I had a bath.

Every puppy is the king of cute!

Cochise Barksdale

The fuss settled down, and the equipment was carried away. I was placed back in my cage and given another snack. I thought that with my up-close-and-personal video ad out in front of the entire television-viewing world, it would be only a short time before proper candidates arrived.

Sure enough, that weekend there were more prospects than usual, but I was not interested in any, until two days later. A guy came down the hall with the attendant, stopping here and there to look at some of the other pups. I played it cool until he was in front of my cage and then went into my routine. He stopped and stuck his finger through the gate. I gave it a sniff, then another sniff, pretending to be reserved, then two big licks! *Sniff, sniff, lick, lick.* In that moment we became drawn to each other. He came in and we paw-boxed—he used two fingers, and I used my front paws. That was all it took; I was convinced and so was he.

Keith filled out some papers while the attendant put me in, of all things, a cat transport box (demeaning but comfortable). A few minutes later we were in his car and off. I was eleven weeks old and being chauffeured into–well, what else, *a dog's life!*

Freedom!

Good Human Companion
Characteristics

To help clarify good human characteristics, I have included in the following pages a list of both good and bad things to look for when choosing a human companion. I do not claim to be an expert, so I enlisted the help of some research by a brilliant dog named Manny Wolf, a chocolate lab and a longtime friend who is a professor at P.I.T University (Puppy Institute of Training). The full study can be obtained from the Psychology Association for Dogs, under the title "Candidate Characteristics and the Pre-Determination of Good Human Companions Versus Bad Human Companions."

RESPONSIBLE:

The root of this word is *response-able*. Dogs need to be taken care of. We need lots of love. We need a human who is able to respond to our love. We need someone to play with, someone who will care for us, someone who will love us. We need a human who is able to respond to the love we give. I know I've written this last sentence twice; it is not an editorial error.

DOG PERSON:

Never go with a cat person. A cat person who has decided to try out a dog in his or her life is not good. We don't do tryouts. A cat-and-dog person is too unstable. They are unable to fully commit, and you'll be subject to comments such as, *We can leave the cat for the weekend, but what are we going to do with the dog?* A dog person is the only way to go. Investigate whether the human has a history of puppy companionship and check references.

Morning person or night person:

Whether you like to get up early in the morning or prefer to sleep late, you're going to want a companion with similar preferences. I am a morning dog, and often I have to wake Keith up to get my morning walk. That is bad enough, but he doesn't just wake up and take me out right away. Instead he wakes up, shuffles around the house, gets a glass of water, takes a shower, gets dressed, makes coffee, eats– Get the picture? And worst of all, then he goes to the bathroom. And I'm standing there busting my bladder! Can you believe that? Hello? Calling the shelter for abused animals! Why does he get to go to the bathroom? Because he can't hold it! Meanwhile, I have all four legs crossed and my eyes are starting to roll back into my head because I need to pee. This is why I woke him up to begin with!

Cochise Barksdale

Active:

You want someone who is about as active as you are. If you are hyper, get a hyper companion. If you are sedate, look for a couch potato. A pairing of opposites is going to be uncomfortable for both of you. I remember an Irish setter named Scotty who never sat down. He would run around the house with his toys, begging his companion to play with him, but the only time the guy even responded was when Scotty got into the line of sight between him and the TV. At times I think Scotty wondered if TV was a rival for the title of *man's best friend*.

Available time for having fun:

It is a published statistic that puppies sleep 90 percent of the time and adult dogs sleep 70 percent of the time. So when my companion gets home, I am ready to play! He may be tired, but I do the *welcome-home-I-missed-you-let's-play-and-run-around-after-I-lick-your-face* happy dance. *Sniff, sniff, lick, lick!* This is the 30 percent of my life when I am awake. Let's have fun! So you need a human who will make time for you, who will play wholeheartedly with you, and who enjoys just hanging out with you.

Affectionate:

The nice thing about being a dog is that we help humans keep alive their inner children. In a simple, less psychological phrase, we can cause most adult humans to act like children. They talk funny to us. Heck, just the fact that they talk to us is funny. Then they use a silly voice and the whole thing gets hilarious. It's cute and endearing. I recommend that you find a companion who talks to you in that funny way or who pets you and cradles your face to tell you how cute you are from time to time. It's a good sign the inner child is alive and well and that they have affection in their hearts.

Playful (a.k.a. full of play):

Once again, I find it useful to break the words down into their components to clearly understand them. In this case, playful is *full of play*. The fountain of youth is defined in dog lore as playing. You want someone who will buy you toys for entertainment, both yours and theirs. I have a small collection of rubber squeaky toys, which includes Mr. Frog, a hamburger, Ms. Bear, and a couple of furry squeaky dolls. These are great; I like to pretend that I am sending a Morse code message to my companion by picking one up and randomly squeaking it while looking him right in the eyes. This always puts a smile on his face, no matter what mood he is in. (Where is Pavlov during these moments? Can you see his study results? *Hmm, we have observed that a human can be conditioned to smile upon the command of a small puppy that squeaks a rubber toy. Curious, but shows promise for the human race's ability to be universally happy.*)

Bad Human Companion Characteristics

Just as there are desirable characteristics for human companions, there are also undesirable ones to avoid. I usually do not stereotype, but these are some broad categories I have noted that puppies should avoid.

The human who is thinking, This one I will train right:

These humans always come on strong with the latest fad in dog obedience training. They are convinced that they are intellectually superior to dogs. Max is a German shepherd friend of mine. His companions, Norm and Penelope, simply refuse to accept their place in the relationship. Max and I listen to them talking about "being an alpha" and "making sure the dog knows who the boss is," and on and on they go. Max humors them when they need it. Poor Max has had a slow time training his humans, but progress is being made. It would be so much simpler if Norm and Penelope, and all humans, would just admit that dogs rule!

The humans who are thinking, We want a dog before having kids:

Be careful of newly married couples if they are using you as a surrogate baby. You will receive lavish attention until they think they are ready to have a puppy of their own—human puppy, that is. Then you might be ignored or worse, restricted about where you can go in the home because they fear you are too big to be around their human puppy. This situation confuses puppies because after a while, there will be so many toys just lying around that it will become difficult to know which ones are yours. And should you chew the wrong toy…not good! How could you have known? Is seems the human puppy can play with your toys just fine and gets all the attention. Nope, we do not do stand-ins for human puppies.

The human who is thinking, Let's get a puppy to teach our child responsibility:

This is simple enough to understand. You see, we puppies are supposed to be the carefree ones! To match us up with a carefree human child is either going to be a lot of fun or a lot of chaos. If it turns out to be chaos, the dog should suggest the parents buy a goldfish for the kid and hire a dog walker. This relates back to the good characteristics; the human must be responsible already, not learning how to be responsible at our expense.

THE HUMAN WHO IS THINKING, I WILL IMPULSIVELY GET A PUPPY:

How many dalmatians found homes because of that movie, *One-Hundred-and-Something Dalmatians?* And how many of them found that when the novelty wore off, the attention and affection also evaporated? Studies have shown that most of the ones adopted were also given to human children to learn responsibility. This violates two of the bad characteristics. Do not select a companion who looks at you as a novelty or a gift for someone else. The sure sign of this intent is if they try to put a bow on your head and see if you fit in a gift basket. Puppies are not an impulse item at the checkout line; we require a ten- to twenty-year commitment to love us, care for us, play with us, and be our companion.

AND OF COURSE, THERE ARE THE INSTANT CANDIDATE REJECTS, SUCH AS WHEN THEY:

• Show up with a chain leash and spiked collar big enough to anchor a boat.

- Arrive in a white surgical gown, mumbling to themselves, especially if their name is Dogtor Frankenstein.

- Wear camouflage and talk about hunting. This means you may have to work for a living and will probably be kept outside and treated like an animal.

- Are concerned about your "papers." This may mean they are thinking of you as an investment. You could end up on the show circuit. Don't get me wrong; it is not a bad life, but it is hard work. And what happens when you pass your prime? Ask any five-year-old greyhound about this. You should not be asked to prance and perform tricks for a panel of judges, retrieve dead birds, or be forced into gambling institutions. You're a dog. Dogs rule; therefore, *we do not work!*

Acceptance Techniques

Once you have the right candidate, you need to close the deal. Here are seven tips for catching a prospect's eye and instantly securing a place in his or her heart:

1. Be alert for new prospects. If you see them first, you will have the edge in getting their attention.

2. Get their attention! Dance, yip, paw, jump, quiver, act cute, do whatever it takes to get them to come to you.

3. Be as clean-smelling as possible.

4. Look them in the eye. Dogtor Barney has concluded that humans can fall in love with a dog after only thirty seconds of uninterrupted eye contact.

5. Give them as many puppy kisses as you can. Remember: *sniff, sniff, lick, lick.*

6. Play with anything they give you.

7. Try not to get so excited that you go wee.

Cochise Barksdale

Sometimes we puppies are faced with having to turn away a bad prospect. The best methods are to act lethargic and sickly or play dead. A little bowwow barf on their shoes means goodbye for sure.

So to summarize these points, in an exercise for you to try, I am including the soon-to-be famous I'm-so-cute-dance song. The song can be sung and danced to any style of music from rap, rock and roll, blues, opera, reggae, or even that funny cartoon-type music.

I'm So Cute Dance

Take a few steps back, it's time to attract.
Do a full-body wiggle wag wild your tail
Start a giant giggle, it just can't fail.

Chorus:

Do the *I'm-cute* dance, just watch me prance.
No human can resist a cute puppy like me
If they dance along, it's meant to be.

Add a little flair and puppy stare,
More *sniff sniff, lick lick,* and *bowwow* too.
Get the human laughing, you know what to do.

Chorus:

Roll over, be silly, and show your belly.
In these few moments if love should show,
You'll both feel love and together you'll go.

Housebreaking Your Human Companion

I was out! I had a companion! And soon I arrived at my new home. Keith had a three-bedroom, two-bath ranch home in Florida. The grounds were large and well landscaped with nice, thick grass. There were nicely curved scrub pine beds lined with mulch and azaleas, which were in bloom and very colorful. The backyard had a screened-in porch with a ten-foot border of grass that swooped toward and away from the home, permitting a flowing feeling, and flowerbeds randomly along the path. Beyond the grass was prime woodland.

I was warned not to go into the woods alone because there could be alligators. I did not even know what an alligator was at the time. But later I found they were definitely something to avoid!

This is a friend, Roxy, with her alligator squeaky.
The real alligators are much larger and not squeaky.

The home sat on a quiet street with about eight other homes. Ours and three more near us were obviously newer than the others; it must have been a dead end at one time that was cut through to the other street to permit four more houses to be built.

When we arrived at the house, Keith carried me up out of the car in his arms and set me down on the grass of the backyard to rest a little and sniff around. After a while, Keith got up and signaled for me to walk with him by patting his thigh excitedly. We started to walk around and slowly got going a little faster and faster and faster until we were in a full run around and around the house. After four laps, Keith rolled down in the grass, and I jumped on his head and crawled on his chest to hold him down. Well, it was really just a cute move. I could not really hold him down; I was just a little puppy.

After our rest, Keith led me to two bowls on the back porch. He removed a bag from his car and fed me my first meal with him. It was the same food I ate in the shelter, but it somehow tasted much better here in my new home. Keith filled the other bowl with fresh water, and I lapped some up, dribbling a little. We lolled away the rest of the afternoon under a huge covered porch.

Our first day together was going great until early evening, when he put me back in the box, carried it into the garage, laid a towel inside for me to be comfortable, and left me. I couldn't believe it! He left me in a box! In the garage! By myself! Oh no, this was not going to last long. The very first day in my new home, and already I had to start training my human companion. Bow wow!

In my best *puppy-in-distress* voice, I spent the next twenty minutes verbalizing my displeasure. I knocked over the box, and eventually Keith opened the door. I did my *I-adore-you-and-I'm-so-cute-you-wouldn't-think-of-leaving-me-in-the-garage-again* dance. It worked like a charm.

Keith carried me into the house. But he also brought that darn box and plopped me inside it again. *Slow learner,* I thought, but patience is the greatest asset when training a human. I leaned against the side of the box and tipped it over, and I was free again! However, Keith took this as a challenge rather than a reality, and he brought in a larger box.

Oh, how stubborn, I thought as he set me back in with the food, towel, and water. He must have read in some canine training manual that dogs do not go to the bathroom in the same place where they sleep. Well, whoever came to that brilliant conclusion deserved to have his research grant renewed so they could record the thought patterns of the brain dead in the first person. Who *would* wee where they sleep? Certainly not a puppy! In fact, I think humans are the only species in the animal kingdom that do wee where they sleep. That is precisely the reason human puppies wear diapers. Yuck!

So there I was in this big box. I was too small to tip it over, and Keith was planning to leave me in the kitchen for the night. What do they say about the best-laid plans of mice and men? They often go to the dogs. This was our first night together. I was not about to spend it alone in a cardboard box.

This puppy in a box with a window to peep out, busy contemplating escape.

We did a few rounds of me yipping and Keith coming in to quiet me and me yipping again once he left. Keith finally gave up, carried the box and me into his bedroom, and set me on the floor next to his bed. Now we were making progress; he was responding very well to training.

It only took a few more minutes of piteous whimpering to make him reach his arm down into the box so I could snuggle up against it. *Sniff, sniff, lick, lick, cuddle, cuddle.* With that I figured he had learned enough for one day, and we both drifted off to a peaceful sleep.

I spent the next week sleeping in that box. Every night Keith hung his arm down for me to fall asleep against. I was growing fast and soon would be big enough to reach the top of the box. Escape was near!

My next tactic was to hook my front paws over the edge of the box and climb by running in place with my rear legs up the inside wall of the box. I was finally successful in tipping the box over, and how was I rewarded? I was put back into the garage! Silly human!

There I was in the garage, a towel spread on the cold cement floor, indicating my new sleeping area. Change was needed, but my yips and yaps were ignored. I think Keith was proceeding on the theory, *If you go to the puppy every time it cries, it will continue to cry whenever it wants you. Therefore, ignore the cries. But check in occasionally to make sure the puppy is not in any real danger.* It was a pity Keith was using such transparent and amateur psychology on me. It only got him more deeply enmeshed in a battle of wits that puppies always win.

During the day I was allowed inside the house but restricted to the kitchen. I understood this since I was developing bladder control, or as human companions like to say, I was being "housebroken." What does that term mean—*housebroken?* I suppose that the dog has been broken from the practice of going potty in the house. This is another delusion suffered by humans. Humans think they are training us to hold our number ones and number twos until we go outside. What they don't understand is that when you are only a few months old, controlling these things is not an intellectual decision or a matter of choice. It's a simple matter of physical inability. (Might I add that human puppies take a lot longer than we do.)

Why are human puppies toilet trained and cats litter-box trained but dogs are housebroken? Shouldn't we be yard trained or curb trained? Regardless of the term, as puppies, we're just like everyone else; when we gotta go, then we gotta go.

Well, Keith banished me to the garage at night and when he was away from the house. I figured if I wanted to get back in the house and start lounging on the sofa, I had to gain his confidence by not going to the bathroom in the house. It took me about a month of practice to attain the necessary control. And then whenever he let me out into the yard, I'd make a big show of weeing on the nearest pine tree (once I figured out that the handrail posts were not good candidates) like I had drunk a bathtub of water. And then I would proudly trot over to the plushest patch of grass on the whole lawn and do a number two.

This went on for a week, and still I was confined to the garage or kitchen. *All right,* I thought, *he needs some more training. And he's going to get it.*

At this point I was having some serious teething issues, and the drive to chew was paramount. In the garage I figured that I could kill two cats with one stone. The door that led into the house was made of wood, a perfectly grained haunch of wood with a firm but delicate texture and the bouquet of fine oak. I started chewing on the trim, then the exposed corner of the door. Naturally, this brought a little discipline my way. I remember his surprise as Keith yelled, "Cochise, you are eating your way through the door!" I just looked at him and sent the telepathic message with appropriate sad and droopy eye contact: *I only want to be with you.*

Eventually, Keith learned that I was determined and finally brought me back into the house before I could chew through the door. As a puppy you sometimes have to be a bit extreme to get the human's attention and make your point. Now that I was in the house full time, I deserved a reward. It was now time to select the piece of furniture that was to become my day bed.

So what am I saying with this story? There is no place we puppies would rather be than with our humans, wherever they may be—following them around the house, lying in bed or on the sofa, walking in the grass. Companions and buddies are supposed to be together; maybe not all the time, but when there is time to do so, do so. How could any human fault us for wanting to be with him or her? Okay, we have to put up with barricades, closed doors, off-limits areas, and boxes, but our unconditional love can overcome any of these in time. *Sniff, sniff, lick, lick.*

Furniture Selection

Five days a week Keith went off to work. I did not fully understand this at the time, but apparently it had something to do with earning a thing called money. Things could be traded for this money such as treats, squeaky toys, and food, so apparently it was something important. While Keith was working I had the house all to myself! This is the time to snooze-test each piece of furniture. I could sleep anywhere—and I did. I never suspected how comfortable it can be to take a nap on something as unlikely as a floral-cloth-covered ottoman when the afternoon sun has warmed it up.

We dogs spend a lot of time sleeping—70

percent of our days, in fact. (Puppies sleep 90 percent of their days!) And I like to sleep on a bed or sofa. Keith tried to keep me off the furniture, which is typical of early-stage trainees.

In the beginning I did not let him see me on any furniture. I only left subtle signs such as hair on the sofa or an indentation on a pillow. He knew I was on the furniture, but he was unable to do anything since it would break the primary rule of dog training, which is "catch them in the act."

As he would leave in the morning I would walk over to the sofa and jump up on it to look out the window. A few times Keith would sneak up on me to see if he could catch me on the sofa or the bed. But he failed to take into account my superior hearing. I can identify Rockports on a mailman from five blocks away, so to me, even in his stocking feet, Keith sounded like a herd of elephants coming down the hallway. I could count his steps and be off the bed and stretched out on the floor half a second before he opened the door every time. He could see the indentation of my body on a cushion, but he could never catch me. Sometimes he would walk over and feel the place where I had just been lying and invariably, it would still be warm. He'd ask me, "Were you on the bed, Cochise?" and then answer himself, "I know you were, you sneaky dog, and I almost caught you." I'd roll over and try to engage him to play; after all, he'd said my name. (If your name is called, you have to assume it is to play.) *Sniff, sniff, lick, lick.*

Of course, he never caught me, ever. And that is the prime rule: *Do not get caught in the act, and your human companion will be unable to do anything.* You can avoid all discipline! Those silly training manuals say humans must be on the scene at the time the dog is engaging in unwanted behavior, otherwise discipline is ineffective and counterproductive. So look cute and radiate love; heck, you can even look guilty. Just don't get caught in the act, or it's discipline time for sure.

Now this is what I call a good dog chaise.

Cochise Barksdale

Furniture time with your human is always good.

Quality time together

The Puppies' Guide to Training Humans

Finally, Keith went from trying to catch me on the furniture to trying to prevent me from being on the furniture. He would stand the sofa cushions on edge to make a kind of wall. With a little effort I was able to get them flat or topple them onto the floor. Either way, they were perfect for an afternoon nap. After some months, Keith finally learned to leave the cushions alone and simply spread a sheet over them just for me. Persistence always overcomes resistance when training people.

I have heard of some human companions who block off portions of the house by closing doors, installing gates, and using furniture to block hallways. These fortifications are utterly ineffective against the ingenuity of a dog.

Eventually the human rationalizes that he or she cannot control you or limit you by simple barriers while he or she is not home. Once this point is reached, the human has accepted, at least subconsciously, that you are on the furniture when he or she is not home. When that has been established, it is time for the next lesson, taking open possession of your furniture.

This requires finesse and infinite aplomb. First, look your human companion gently in the eye as you sit near the piece of furniture you intend to claim. Project the feeling that you wish to sit up on it but are not sure you should. Next, rest your chin or a front paw on the piece of furniture to test for any reaction. After a few minutes, if there is no response, go for it. One short, self-assured leap, and you are there. Curl up quickly, get comfortable, look directly at your human companion, and ooze contentment. I found that a deep inhale and slow relaxing exhale through the nose was a perfect audible indication that I was comfortable.

If your human companion is a slow learner, he or she may try to chase you off the first few times. But if you have been consistent in applying my principles up to this point, your human will know (at least on a subconscious level) who the boss really is. He or she will put up only token resistance, enough to keep up appearances and stroke his or her delicate ego. That piece of furniture—indeed, every piece of furniture—is yours! Enjoy them.

You may even find that your human companion will give you your own special blanket to put on the furniture. Keith used to set up what I call *decoy beds*. These ranged from a sheet on the floor to a cedar-chip, beanbag-type thing made for dogs (or so they claim). The intent was to get me comfortable on something other than the furniture. Funny how I never saw *Keith* sitting or sleeping on any of these decoys. He would sit on the sofa and try to get me interested in a sheet fluffed up on the wooden floor. This was not giving me much credit for intelligence.

The final phase of furniture selection is sharing a sofa or bed with your companion and cuddling. Whether you're lying on the sofa with your human and watching a movie or just stretched out on the bed at night, cohabitation of the same piece of furniture is the ultimate accomplishment in furniture appropriation. *Sniff, sniff, lick, lick, cuddle.*

It is most easily accomplished with the tried-and-true, *be-cute-to-get-what-you-want* routine. Simply focus your big, sweet eyes on your human companion's eyes. Look somewhat upward, as this helps simulate humility. Place your paw on his or her arm or leg as if you want to be petted. After a minute or two of this heart-melting behavior, bring your nose to rest on the cushion. When instinct says the time is ripe, place one paw up, wait a moment, then place your other paw up on the cushion. While still maintaining the petting, slowly but with iron determination, inch your chest and stomach up on the cushion or bed. The toughest part of the act is to momentarily appear to struggle. Claw and flail gently with your hind legs once or twice. That is all it will usually take for your human companion to reach out and help you up.

"Hello, I am right here between your knees, looking to get up on the sofa with you."

Before anyone realizes what has happened, your back legs will have found their way up, and you will be lying comfortably on the couch or bed with your head on your human companion's lap. Reward your human companion with your most loving cuddle, and you will be home free.

Housecleaning

As a puppy, you have certain advantages a grown dog does not have, such as the teething process. I used this stage to do some housecleaning by chewing up some ratty old sneakers, forcing Keith to get a new pair. I trained him to pick up after himself by chewing to bits anything he left lying around the house.

The exposed wood of old, unsightly furniture is another good choice for some selective teething. This will condition your human companion to keep your house clean and your furnishings up to date.

One word of caution: use discretion in what

you chew. I do not recommend feminine shoes with Italian labels. I made this mistake once. My defense to Keith was, "I'm a dog. I cannot tell the difference between a rawhide bone and a leather high heel."

Keith's defense to his girlfriend was, "It is not the dog's fault; you have to be careful where you leave your shoes."

Red shoes, bad choice to chew, but she never left them lying around again.

Cochise Barksdale

Neither defense worked. Keith's girlfriend was so upset that he and I ended up in the doghouse for two days, and Keith had to buy a replacement pair of shoes. Hell truly hath no fury like a woman shorn—of her Guccis, that is! That was some good-tasting leather, though. Unfortunately, she never left her shoes lying around again. She was quickly trained.

Outside

Although we enjoy the comforts found inside a home, outdoors is a world of adventure and play. All a human companion has to say is "out," and we all react the same—we do our *let's-go-outside* dance. Fresh air to breathe, squirrels and cats to chase, sticks to chew, trees to pee on, scraps to feast on—the best adventures in life are found *outside!* I admit that on cold or rainy days it does feel good to be cozy and warm, sitting by the fireplace with my head on someone's lap. But normally, we *love* being outside!

Whether you are a city dog limited to concrete sidewalks, small parks, and—I hate to even use the words—*dog runs,* or a country dog with miles of grass and woods for your outdoor pleasure, here are some time-tested tricks for extending that all-important outdoor time.

The first rule is to always show interest and enthusiasm for anything remotely connected with going outside. It's easy to make humans feel guilty. If you can make them think they've disappointed you, it might be good for an extra walk. For example, whenever I see someone putting on shoes and/or a coat, I get excited and naturally assume the purpose is to go outside with me. And if I hear car keys jingle I am at the door in an instant, waiting to join whoever is leaving, no matter where they might be going. A few pleading glances, a whimper or two, and they think I need to go out.

Once someone decides to take me out, I'm through the door, down the stairs, and doing the happy-body tail-wiggle all the way. But getting out is only half the battle; the other half is staying out until you're good and ready to come in.

This is when all those lessons on bladder control, learned as a puppy and perfected by constant practice, come into play. The comedian

George Carlin did a standup routine in which he explains to his daughter that a dog goes number one and number two. She takes the dog out, comes back, and says it went number eight, meaning four ones and two twos. Don't make the easy mistake of going all at once. Dogs are still hunters at heart, and we have to mark our territory. Once you get outside, pee a little but hold on to that number two. If you let it go too early, your human companion will think you are finished and prematurely end your time outside.

Humans know you have to do number two, and they will wait for you. I used to fake it a few times so Keith thought I was really trying. I would grunt, strain, and look disappointed. Just keep peeing—a little squirt here and a little squirt there. This will extend the outdoor time and accustom the human companion to your need for plenty of time outside. There is a fine line, however. Human companions will eventually lose their patience with all the sniffing, especially if they think you are faking. But we are dogs and that's what we do; we sniff almost everything—including other dogs' butts!

If possible, head directly away from the house and keep going for as long as you can. Beware of the once-around-the-block walk, which is a circular tour timed to get you back where you started in just a few minutes. The first time your human companion tries this on you, hold your business until you finish the lap, let a little pee go, and then start sniffing with a focused urgency, moving away from the house all the time. At the very worst, this will get your human companion to enlarge the circle. When you feel you have maximized the length of the walk, do number two. Over time, your human companion will get used to the fact that number two comes last and that it takes considerable effort to find just the right conditions.

Another method for extending outdoor time is to train your human companion to play your favorite game. Some of us are ball players, some are stick chasers, and some with unusual coordination are even into Frisbee (they are usually showing off for the girl). Don't wait for your human companion to suggest a game; show some initiative. Grab a great stick, drop it right in front of his or her feet, look up, and hang your tongue out and pant while wagging your tail. I guarantee he will throw it a couple of times. Sometimes Keith tries to fake me out by only pretending to throw the stick and then watching me run for nothing. All dogs know the joke is on the human. We don't care about sticks; we just want to be outside playing! And besides, there is always a real throw after the fake one. This is a sign that your human companion is enjoying the play. Dogs help humans stay young at heart by having them play. Mission accomplished!

The old hide-the-stick-behind-your-back routine; isn't my human cute?

But eventually there is a toss for us to chase.

Cats are a wonderful diversion. We know that when we are off the leash, we are supposed to stay within sight. But we all have natural instincts that we can't fight. There are cats in every neighborhood. If you pick up the scent, immediately crouch low to the ground. Your human companion will think this is really cute, as if we are acting on some kind of primal instinct. Keith called this "sleeping tiger in the grass."

Next, launch yourself toward the intended victim. Pretend you do not hear your human screaming, "No!" Then he or she will rationalize your behavior. You were incited—victimized, even—by that snotty cat. The ploy here, of course, is that none of us is interested in cats. They have razor claws and are not any fun to wrestle with, but they are a good excuse for a fast, hard run. Squirrels or anything else that moves work just as well. Even other puppies are great to play with, but be sure you pick one with a good attitude. I once made the mistake of jumping to play with a basset hound. He looked lazy and fun, but let me tell you, that hound had no sense of humor. He howled and snarled and chased my butt around the park several times until he realized I was much faster. Okay, maybe it was a little fun, only because the fat basset could not catch me.

If you are lucky, you have an athletic human companion, and he or she may jog to stay in shape. This type of human loves to run, and you love to run. Convince your human companion to take you along; it's a win-win situation. Be careful, though, if your human companion is a serious runner. Those people are crazy. They will go out in all weather, and they run much farther than any sane dog would care to go. So if your human companion is not training for a marathon, wait until he or she dons a jogging outfit and sneakers, then stand near the door, wag the old tail, and bark until he or she agrees to take you along. It will become a routine.

These times are great for bonding—just the two of you out in the fresh air. The only negative aspect of this type of trip is that you don't get to stop and sniff as much as you would on a normal walk. This can be overcome by running ahead, sniffing until your human companion catches up, and then repeating. This is called the *advance scout routine.* Humans think it is based on an instinct to check out the path ahead for danger. We are scouting all right, not for danger, but for good things to smell— and the random edible!

"Okay, it is safe up here; just a stick, and I got it!"

Cochise Barksdale

*"How do I do this without a thumb and
without getting my paws wet?"*

Naturally, real, quality outdoor time is spent off the leash. I am a city dog, and this is a treat for me. In order to get your human companion to let you off the leash, you must make him or her feel that he or she is still in complete control, even when you are running free. Here are my seven tips for getting off the leash:

1. Never pull—this gives the impression that you need to be restrained; your human companion will pull back.

2. Always prance playfully immediately after being released to show your human companion how much you enjoy the freedom.

3. Stay nearby unless you have an excuse—such as a cat, dog, stick, squirrel, tree, bush, food, person, leaf, or hallucination—on which to blame your lapse in good behavior.

4. Never fight with other dogs, never chase strangers, and never scare children.

5. Never wander too far out of sight, and never stray out of hearing or smelling range. You never know when your human will decide to eat a sandwich or something he or she will consider sharing with you.

6. Always return, eventually, when called. (You can delay a little by blaming it on poor hearing, or a cat, or another dog, or food you found, or anything, but there is a time limit before the human gets impatient or upset that you are not returning.)

7. Always show a lot of love. Remember that positive reinforcement is the best way to encourage repeat behavior.

Cochise Barksdale

Being outside is fun, but it is not where we want to *live*. Be careful of the extreme human companion who believes we are supposed to be "outdoor animals." This is the human companion who has a doghouse in the backyard and thinks it is just dandy for us to have all that open air and freedom to roam.

Caesar, a friend of mine in Atlanta, has to live like this. His human companion is Mike, an otherwise kind man. He leaves Caesar outside with only a doggie door into the garage. (At least there is shelter if needed.) But Mike also believes in self-feeding doggie dishes and trickle adapters on the water faucet. This means Caesar has to suck his water like a hamster, and he never gets to leverage a long face at mealtime into extra goodies from the table.

In short, Caesar lives like an animal. No doubt Mike loves Caesar, but this kind of treatment is a natural result of the outdoor-dog mentality, which you want to avoid at all costs. Caesar, like any of us, would like to be lounging on Mike's king-size bed at night, rather than curled up on the ivy in the yard or in his "dog" house, which brings up the subject of doghouses in general.

Some humans believe a doghouse is a good place for us to stay, but when they use the term among themselves, it does not sound so positive. So I looked it up in their dictionary. *Doghouse,* or more accurately, *being in the doghouse,* is defined as *a state of disfavor.* Why, if a doghouse is not a good place for humans, would they want us to consider staying in one? Simple—they never were literally inside one. They use it as a figure of speech because when they think about it, the doghouse is only big enough for us to fit inside. It is usually dirty (no maid service), and the front yard is often muddy or a dirt bowl because of the lack of landscaping. In short, it is a slum shack, not a doghouse! There are no windows to look out of, no furniture to lie on. Heck, there isn't even a door for us to close for privacy. Humans don't want to live in a doghouse; how can they expect us to live there?

A doghouse should be defined as *the place where the human companion has decided to live with his or her dog, with soft furniture, a comfortable atmosphere, and plenty of toys!*

I have written to the dictionary companies with this recommendation and am still waiting for a reply.

Doghouse, front yard, food and water bowls, empty.
He's inside the home on the sofa (where else?).

Now with all that said, there is something else
to understand about humans: their reaction to
inclement weather. Humans have a strange attitude
toward wind, rain, and snow. They act as though the
weather hurts them. If you want to stay out and play
in the rain, special tactics are required. Humans feel
that any weather but clear skies and sunshine is an
inconvenience. (They have so much to learn from
us.) A spontaneous run in the rain rejuvenates the

senses and nurtures the puppy in us all. I love wet grass on my paws, splashing in deep puddles, and rolling in the mud. It makes me feel alive and young!

On wet and rainy days after your outside time, you should loosen your human companion up a little. Right after stepping inside the front door, shake your coat vigorously. It is best to wait until your human companion takes off his or her raincoat so the water shake's effectiveness is maximized. All human companions know this is coming, but somehow it always takes them by surprise. They are cute creatures, though a tad predictable. *Sniff, sniff, lick, lick.*

Humans do have a way of sometimes including us too much in their lifestyle. Just when things were getting really comfortable for me in my midlife, Keith decided to buy a sailboat. This might sound wonderful—sailing out on the open water, wind, sun, and new people to play with. Well, it's not, in my opinion, how the romance writers describe it as being.

I must admit that the first time I was invited, I was thrilled. You know the moves. First it's the hyper jumping around, then the tail wagging, and the tongue hanging out—the whole *yeah-I-want-*

to-get-out-of-the-house routine. Then it's in the car and to the dock. *Freedom at last! But hold on! What's this bright orange thing being strapped around my body? A life jacket? I don't think so! How am I supposed to look cool with this goofy thing on?*

"I'm trying to look cool in this life-jacket; hope a cat does not see me."

Of course, I soon realized that without it I would have to do the doggie paddle for quite some distance to get to dry land. Also, it served as an excellent body pillow. It really wasn't so bad once I realized I would be sliding from side to side on the floor of the boat.

For those of you who don't sail, let me tell you from a dog's perspective that it's no hike in the woods. First, I have to step off the solid ground to a wobbly dock, then onto a boat that moves around even more. Finally, I find a place to wedge myself on board and we leave the dock. Okay, this is nice—cool breeze blowing, sun shining, all's right with the world, and I am with my human.

But just when I get comfortable, we change direction and I am sliding to the other side of the boat. And there are no soft couches here that I could keep myself from falling off. We're talking wood and fiberglass seats with a flotation cushion on the floor for a little softness. Next time I might stay in the yacht club lounge with that cute little dog on the boat across the dock.

Hiking and camping. Now these are activities Keith should do more of. I can't think of a better way to spend my weekend. First, it's the car ride to the woods. Then it's a day filled with activities dogs like best—walking in the woods freely with no annoying leash, chasing squirrels to my heart's content, scouting ahead to keep my group on track (no need for those little markers on the trees; I can follow any trail by scent), and then nights spent under the stars. (Well, I really slept in a tent. I do prefer a soft bed or couch to the ground, but we were roughing it.)

Keith has this thing about responsibility, and for some reason he thinks that I should carry my own food and water. And some smart son of a gun happens to have invented a doggy backpack. Very cute! But I figured that if I was going to be invited back, I should not complain about having to haul a little of my own gear.

Peeking out from under the tent to see if breakfast is ready.

A hike, a run, and a stick game with my human companion—this is a great day!

Cochise Barksdale

Quiet reflection, sitting in the beautiful countryside, just me and my human.

Now the other extreme is being carried. I am a fairly large dog, and carrying my own food and water was kind of cool and made me feel like a team member. But there is another point of view for you smaller puppies.

I was in Breckenridge, Colorado, one summer when I met Juanita, Margarita, Bonita, and Señorita, four chihuahuas. These four friends of mine had elevated hiking to a new level of luxury. Their human companions were very sympathetic to the fact that the chihuahuas had very short legs and therefore very short strides. They had to move their legs like hummingbirds to keep up with their humans on a hike. The ratio, Margarita explained to me, was about twenty of her steps to one of their humans'. Then there were the obvious height difficulties to overcome, such as getting over logs, rocks, and holes. So to make the hike more enjoyable for the whole family, their humans adapted two kiddy backpacks, one in front on their chest and one on their back. Each of the humans carried two of my friends so they could keep up. When they reached a field or suitable play area, they would let the chihuahuas out to romp around and play. Now that is training extraordinaire! That is the way to go. I wonder if Keith would consider a Sudan chair for me on our next hike.

Cochise Barksdale

Food—What Is "Original Flavor"?

Humans have mistakenly adopted the belief (thanks in part to the commercial dog food industry) that a steady diet of the same bland food is a good thing. I have heard pet professionals explain that changing our diet can cause stomach problems and we certainly should not be given "people" food. Actually, we do have some adverse effects from a change in diet, but this is only due to the excitement caused by the aroma and taste of real food.

There are facts about people food that is bad for us puppies. I will cover them here so you know, just in case your human does not and tries to feed you some of them by accident.

- Alcoholic beverages can cause gastrointestinal irritation (I think that means farting), drunkenness, tremors, difficulty breathing and/or panting, coma, and even death. Although, I like a few laps of champagne on the New Year's Eve celebration.

- Avocados can result in respiratory distress and the accumulation of fluid around the heart.

- Bones—small bones that can splinter and get stuck in our throat or stomach are bad. We like big shoulder bones, and ask your human to leave a little meat on them.

- Chocolate can cause vomiting, diarrhea, seizures, hyperactivity, and increased thirst, urination, and heart rate.

- Coffee (including the grounds and beans) can cause the same symptoms as chocolate. I am too hyper anyway.

Cochise Barksdale

- Corn is completely indigestible and holds no value for us or humans.

- Grapes and raisins, depending on the amount ingested: clinical signs can range from vomiting to life-threatening kidney failure.

- Macadamia nuts contain an unknown compound, but the effect of macadamia nuts is to cause difficulty in walking and orientation as if drunk.

- Onions, if eaten in excess, can kill us. They also cause dog breath, which is bad for kissing other dogs and humans.

- Salt and salty foods can result in sodium ion poisoning with symptoms of regurgitation, tremors, excessive thirst, diarrhea, high temperature, and seizures. On the other hand, moderate amounts of natural salt can be healthy.

- Tomato is not a problem in moderation, but the leaves, stem, and unripe tomatoes are. Ingestion of these can cause gastrointestinal upset, excess salivation, drowsiness, dilated pupils, and weakness. The same symptoms can be seen with the ingestion of any green plant parts of the potato and many household plants.

- Xylitol sweetener in candies and gum can also cause a fairly sudden drop in blood sugar, resulting in depression and seizures. But I cannot read those ingredient lists anymore without glasses. Do you think they print that stuff small on purpose?

- Yeast dough can be double trouble in that as it rises, the dough can expand the gastrointestinal tract, possibly causing the intestine to rupture. The yeast can also form alcohol as it rises, leading to alcohol poisoning. Really, who wants to eat yeast dough? Cookie dough absolutely, however!

- Then there are the common-sense items. Puppies, stay away from moldy food, rotten food, antifreeze, cleaning products, and all household chemicals and drugs. Some of these substances (such as antifreeze) actually taste good but can cause serious illness and death. Okay, if any of you puppies are eating this stuff, there is some other problem, like starvation. Speak to your companion about more food, even if it is just nuggets, and follow my training for how to get the humans to feed you some of the variety mentioned later in this chapter. Please do not eat or drink bad stuff.

- Be sure to use caution with spicy foods, cooked bones, and virtually any commercial product fed continuously. Again, the principle to keep in mind is that variety is the spice of health. Since anything can potentially be toxic if fed in excess, varying the diet is the best safeguard.

- Poop—I saved this for last, but really, those of you who eat poop. Stop it!

Most human companions are afraid of changing our diet because we may have diarrhea. Others consider a change in food to be necessary only for the transition from puppy food to dog food to senior food. Or sometimes your usual brand is out of stock and your human companion is forced into a short-term change. Humans just do not understand the simple truth: anyone who eats the same thing in the morning, afternoon, and night, day after day, week after week, year after year will welcome a change, even if it is a piece of moldy pizza crust on the floor.

If humans picked their favorite food and had to eat that single food and nothing else for breakfast, lunch, dinner, and snacks, they would not last a week without adding some variety. What is amazing is the shallow thought that goes into what some human companions call *variety*. Dog treats and dog biscuits, for instance, are usually the same hard food in different shapes and colors. Another great example of a human's idea of variety is alternating wet and dry food and occasionally mixing the two. Well, that is like alternating dry cereal and oatmeal and occasionally making cement out of the two combined. Yuck, not exactly canine cuisine extraordinaire! No *lick, lick, sniff, sniff!*

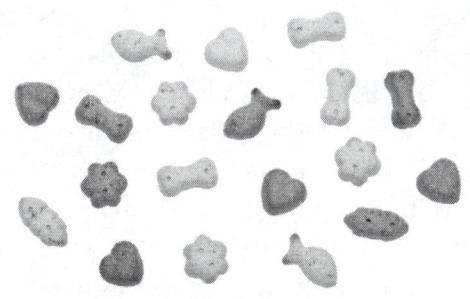

Treats—they are just the same stuff as nuggets but in different shapes. Why do they call them treats!

I am not happy about nuggets for dinner again. For three years I have been eating the same thing! Can't I have something else?

The Puppies' Guide to Training Humans

Then there are the "flavored" foods: chicken-flavored, beef-flavored, liver-flavored, beef-and-cheese-flavored, and my favorite, original flavor. What is *original* flavor? It is not the taste of raw flesh or Mama's doggie breast milk; it is the first taste the dog food company decided to manufacture. This begs the following question: Who did the taste-testing at the manufacturing plant? I have never heard of a taste-test panel of dogs. Have you ever seen a sample-platter person in the dog food aisle at the grocery store offering samples on toothpicks to dogs passing by to get their feedback? Nope, never! So who is doing the decision making?

Raw meat—now this is what we carnivores call original flavor, but this is too much work to chew.

*Doggie mommy milk—yum yum—is also original fla-
vor. What are those people in the pet-food marketing
thinking when they call a can of yuck original flavor?*

The operative word with all this food is
flavored. It is nothing but the same junk with a
different flavor and color. It is not chicken; it is the
same old dog food flavored to taste like chicken.
I bet humans never even read the ingredients on
those cans as they do with their own food.

This required a little investigation. I rounded
up a few cans of food to review the ingredients–

yuck! I would rather eat my furry squeaky toy than what is in that can pretending to be dog food! Let me share with the rest of you dogs what the humans are trying to feed us. I will not disclose the brand, but it is safe to say that most brands use the same general ingredients, which sound like what is swept off the floor of some disgusting factory.

Chunky, with Beef.

Ingredients: water, meat byproduct, chicken, beef, soy flour, poultry byproduct, sodium, tripolyphosphate, potassium chloride, carrageenan, locust bean gum, salt, natural flavor, guar gum, caramel color.

The rest is a bunch of chemicals and vitamin additives. What are *meat byproduct* and *poultry byproduct?* Back to the human dictionary: *byproduct* is defined as *something produced in addition to the principal product, a secondary and sometimes unexpected or unintended result.* Maybe this is where the *chunky* comes from? When I pawed through the dictionary to look up the word *meat,* I actually found the full term *meat byproduct*. Ready? Well, hold on to your stomach! The definition is *a usable product other than flesh obtained from slaughtered animals.* Puke!

Let me continue to the final analysis. Every dog should also be aware of the fat content of food. The same can of food I described above has the following breakdown:

- Crude protein—minimum 9.0 percent
- Crude fat—minimum 5.0 percent (Looking good so far—low fat!)
- Crude fiber—maximum 1.5 percent
- Moisture—maximum 78.0 percent
- Calcium—minimum 0.22 percent

I know I am a dog, but I was not aware that *moisture* was one of the four basic food groups. And what exactly is *crude?* Back to the dictionary. (It's a good thing I can read!) *Crude* is defined as *existing in a natural state and unaltered by cooking or processing.* In other words, *raw protein, fat, and fiber!*

That clears it up! This particular dog food is raw, undefined animal chunks from the slaughter process! No way I am eating this stuff, even if my human companion eats it first. The scraps in the garbage can are looking rather appetizing in comparison.

Here is the best line on the entire can of Chunky, with Beef: *Animal feeding tests using AAFCO procedures substantiate that [brand name] Chunky, with Beef provides complete and balanced nutrition for the growth and maintenance of dogs.*

This required a little Web research. (It's a good thing I know how to use a computer!) I typed *AAFCO* into the search engine, and sure enough, up pops Association of American Feed Control Officials. I looked through its board of directors and members, and just as I suspected, there was not one dog listed. I will concede that the organization has a somewhat reasonable purpose: *The basic goal of AAFCO is to provide a mechanism for developing and implementing uniform and equitable laws, regulations, standards, and enforcement policies for regulating the manufacture, distribution, and sale of animal feeds; resulting in safe, effective, and useful feeds.*

No mention there about tasty! Could you imagine human food being described as *safe, effective, and useful?*

Then there are the other types: Chunky, with Beef, Bacon, and Cheese, and the Prime Cuts in Gravy with Chicken and Rice. In addition to the ingredients listed in Chunky, with Beef, there was "cheese meal" in the Chunky, with Beef, Bacon, and Cheese and "animal plasma" in the Prime Cuts. I am not even interested in looking up those terms in the dictionary.

But in my search for AAFCO, I found a few other listings that interested me. I'll share them here so those dogs without Internet access can be fully informed.

First, there is the list of AAFCO dog food definitions, which listed:

meat byproducts—the non-rendered, clean parts, other than meat, derived from slaughtered mammals. It includes but is not limited to lungs, spleen, kidneys, brain, livers, blood, bone, partially defatted, low-temperature fatty tissue and stomachs and intestines freed of their contents. It does not include hair, horns, teeth, and hooves.

Only a few of the other terms on the dog food cans were listed there, which I suppose means the company can make up its own definitions.

The next thing that was interesting was the AAFCO dog-food-testing procedures. For adult maintenance dog food to pass the AAFCO test, the following must be true:

- Eight dogs older than one year must start the test.

- At start, all dogs must be normal weight and health.

- A blood test is to be taken from each dog at the start and finish of the test.

- For six months, the dogs used must eat only the food being tested.

- The dogs finishing the test must not lose more than 15 percent of their body weight.

- During the test, none of the dogs used is to die or be removed because of nutritional causes.

- Six of the eight dogs starting must finish the test.

"Yes, hello Puppy Pizza. I would like to order one large carnivore pizza, for delivery, please."

That's all there is to it! I am not saying all commercial food is like this. During the last ten years I have noted premium and gourmet *human-quality* food for us being put on the market, which is a better choice of evils. But basically, using a little human irony, all this stuff is *dog* food! This is no way to live.

We are natural carnivores, after all. Thousands of years ago, we lived in the wild and hunted our own food. Not that we want to go that route anymore, but a juicy steak with some gravy, a good slice of veal, or some leftover chicken is always welcome. Brothers and sisters, I know you have dreams about good food the way I do. Let's explore sources of enriching your diet.

I conducted a survey that concluded that 70 percent of the humans requesting a doggie bag at the end of the meal for their leftovers are going to eat the food themselves, 15 percent intend to eat it themselves but leave it at the restaurant, and 10 percent intend to eat it themselves but end up throwing it out. That means 95 percent of all doggie bags are not going to the doggie! Hello-o-o! Something is wrong here!

Through some historical research I have been able to detect that the origin of the "doggie bag" was started by a Victorian upper-class woman who was too embarrassed to say she wanted her leftovers to take home and eat herself. So she quietly asked the waiter to place the remains in a bag for her foo-foo poodle. That poodle saw none of it! *Webster's New Collegiate Dictionary* defines *doggie bag* as *the presumption that such leftovers are intended for a pet dog; a bag used for carrying home leftover food and especially meat from a meal eaten at a restaurant.* The key word is *presumption.*

So how do we do it? How do we get a more robust menu to choose from? I've picked up many techniques for adding more flavorful items to my cuisine. A source of great variation is those unexpected finds on the streets and sidewalks discovered during routine walks. The key here is to spot the item without letting my companion know the reason for the diversion. I casually sniff in a certain direction, and as soon as I'm within snatching distance, I wolf down the gourmet item. *Sniff, sniff, lick, gulp!* Usually it's a piece of bread or cookie dropped by children. If I'm really lucky and am having a good day, I can feast on pizza crust or restaurant leftovers.

Of course, after I've eaten I have to hear the same old speech: "Cochise, stop eating garbage," or "You're such a trash hound." Well, obviously, if I had some variety in my diet I wouldn't have to stoop to eating off the street. Please look at the stuff I was being fed every single meal. *Yuck!* Human companions do not understand that if we ate like they do, we would not have to eat scraps off the ground.

The key to unlock this dilemma is that most human companions believe that human food is not good for us. Hey, come on, most human food is not good for humans. I am not interested in a hot dog or some other processed mush that is only differentiated from dog food by its shape and marketing. I am talking about a nice piece of beef, chicken fillet, occasional pasta, and my favorite, bread in any form. How can human companions believe this is not good for us? We were originally carnivores that hunted down other animals before we decided to tame humans to be our companions.

Don't give dogs scraps from the table because they will get used to it and beg is another ignorant statement. Let's look at this piece by piece. *Don't give the dog scraps.* I agree, don't give me scraps either—I expect a full portion of my own. This is the same line of thought that leads to *Don't give dogs chicken bones because they can choke on them.* Very true, this is no myth. But who in their right mind eats chicken bones? Take the meat off the bone and give it to me, or make my day with a boneless chicken breast. We do not like to eat bones. But we are so grateful for the ability to eat something that we will gnaw at the bones to get as much of the taste as possible. Sometimes in our excitement we chew a bone to splinters. But I digress.

Let's look at the rest of the line: *from the table.* Most books human companions read on dog training state that if we are fed from the table, we will associate the food with the table and will be prone to begging there. These books suggest giving scraps to the dog well after the meal has been completed. Who do they think they are dealing with? We do not care *when* we get the food; we only care *if* we get the food. I strongly recommend locating yourself near the table in a quiet but obvious manner as a reminder to save some food. Also, if you hang out during the cooking process, the human companion may just prepare a little too much or give you a sample.

The last part of the line is *because they will get used to it and beg.* Oh, come on! We should not have to *beg!* We should not be given the same food over and over again! What is wrong with getting used to eating a variety of food? Plus, we are not begging; we are teaching. Begging is just another dominant human term to support their frail egos. We are educating the human companion that it would be far nobler of them to feed us some variety. Begging is to plead to others for something they have which you need. This is not what we are doing. We are not pleading; we are increasing our human companions' awareness.

"I am not begging. I am just viewing some food that might come my way after dinner. Heck, I will even share with the cat, I am so big hearted."

One of the things I used to do that worked great was to not eat my bowl of food until Keith finished his meal and cleaned up. First of all, during mealtime, I was sending my *hungry* glance at him, trying to obtain whatever scrap I could. But the great guilt move was that once the meal was done, I would walk over to my bowls and lap some water to cleanse my palate and prepare the digestive tract for the hard, flavored nuggets. I would eat my whole bowl. Eventually, Keith realized that I only ate after he did and would place leftovers on top of my bowl of nuggets. Occasionally, a little gravy or tomato sauce would be ladled over my food. Slowly, gestures like these were made routine, and my diet improved.

Occasionally, I would eat only the leftovers off the top with great enthusiasm and then pause for a few minutes while looking around for more. I would then stare at Keith, lick my lips, and slowly go back and eat the nuggets. This little interlude is a great guilt builder and occasionally is good for more leftovers that were destined for the refrigerator.

Attention Antics and Tactics

It is especially good to use a squeaky toy to get attention. When I squeak a toy, no matter how upset my human companion may be, he always smiles.

Many of us feel that our human companions do not spend enough time with us. We are social creatures and often like to be the center of attention. Granted, we sleep around 70 percent of the time, but when we are awake we want to play. Sometimes we have to get our human companion's attention by barking, sniffing, licking, pawing, staring, standing, hugging, gassing, or "bed runs."

Barking is the most common attention-getting move we have. It is age old, but in the right circumstances, still very effective. Sophisticated barking at the right moment can be just what you need to redirect your human companion's focus. There are three basic types of barks: (1) the half bark, or woof, (2) the multiple barks, and (3) the yip.

The most effective bark is the half bark, also called a woof, followed by a series of tail wagging and prancing. The woof sound is made by muffling a full bark; that is, by closing the mouth halfway through the bark, which lowers the volume and exclamatory nature of a full bark.

Repetitive barks become annoying, not to mention are hard on the vocal cords, and should be used only in extreme situations. I don't like barking for too long. What will the neighbors think? Usually if you bark too long, human companions think they need to ignore you and you will stop, or they feel there is something wrong and you need their help. The irony of this second angle is that the human capacity to understand what is wrong is fairly limited. For example, I was chained to a tree in the backyard on several occasions. How barbaric! After about fifteen minutes of solid barking, Keith came out to see what the matter was. He went back in after thinking nothing was wrong (his opinion only). So I had to bark for five minutes more before he returned. *Nothing wrong?* I thought to myself. *Nothing except this chain connecting me to a tree!* What would happen in an emergency? What if a cat came by and saw me? I would lose all self-respect and be the object of feline mockery. After a while, Keith finally improved his behavior and let me loose. After all, I only wanted to hang out with him!

Yipping is the higher-pitched bark typical of small dogs. Yipping is very annoying and quite effective in making the human companion completely unable to focus on anything else. Like barking, yipping is fine for extreme situations.

The main thing to keep in mind when barking is not to cry wolf. This means that you should not bark unless you have a good reason; otherwise, people will stop paying attention to you when you do bark. I might suggest an update to this cliché, which is, "Don't cry, just woof." This means do not whimper about a situation; just give a cute woof to get some attention.

Of course, there are many other ways to effectively gain attention other than barking. I would often just follow Keith around the house or outside. Wherever he went, I went. Sometimes he would stop short and I would walk into him. How cute can I be?

When he would settle in somewhere, I would settle in nearby. When he got up and started walking, I got up and started following. After all, he could be going to the bedroom, where I could lie on the bed, or the kitchen for food, or outside. I was not going to miss anything.

Sniffing and using your nose is good also for attention. I used to tap and tip things with my nose to indicate I wanted something. I would open almost-shut doors, using my nose as a wedge, and sniff at the door when I heard Keith coming home. He would hear me as he unlocked the door, knowing that his greeting committee—I—was excited to see him. And you can use your nose to leave cute reminders of yourself, such as nose prints on the window of your home or car. Nose tunneling is standard procedure as well for getting stroked. This is a simple maneuver by which you take your nose and lift up your human's hand or arm so that it is on top of your head. This helps him or her get his or her hand in the right position for stroking you.

Licking is good, real good. *Sniff, sniff, lick, lick.* I can sometimes lick a hand or thigh for ten minutes or more. No one can withstand that. The humans think this is because we need salt, but it is simply our way of being affectionate and getting some attention.

Sniff, sniff, lick, lick. Puppy breath and all, we are too cute!

The Puppies' Guide to Training Humans

Pawing a leg or an arm and pulling it toward you is good too. Be careful not to have muddy paws or to leave a mark on the good clothing of your human companion.

Staring. Ah, staring. Nothing can be more heartwarming than the direct long stare of big brown puppy eyes. Occasionally, Keith would lie on the sofa and watch a movie or read a book. After following him to the room, I would settle in with a long inhale and audible exhale through the nose. Then I would position my head to rest on both my front paws and lock eyes on Keith. Every time he looked at me, I was staring at him. Sometimes he would try to engage me in a staring contest. But eventually he would melt and would think I was too cute, and he'd ask me to jump up on the sofa with him and cuddle or even come over to me, give me a big hug, and lie on the floor with me. Mission accomplished!

Ah, no one can resist my puppy eyes.

I would also combine staring with a squeaky toy. Stare while squeezing the toy to make its sound, and you are practically guaranteed attention. Or try holding the toy or your leash and staring. This is also very powerful, bound to put a smile on the human's face and affection in his or her heart.

Hind-leg standing, particularly the rear-leg stand, is usually reserved for small dogs such as Jack Russell terriers or poodles. Heck, some poodles would act as though they went to ballet classes the way they could get around on their hind paws. I was never very good at this, but Twix, a golden retriever, was great at it, especially for his size. Twix could walk ten feet or more on his hind legs, like a human, even on a wood-planked deck!

The full-body hug is good for medium to large dogs but works just as well for small dogs, although it is more of a full-leg hug. It is not recommended for the giant breeds, such as great danes. A friend of mine, Otto, who happens to be a great dane, stood up and placed his paws on his human companion's shoulders one day and started to lick his face. The human companion fell backward from the weight, while Otto stayed on top of him, still licking. Otto nearly suffocated him!

Hugging us is always good. Dogtors say
we bring energy to the older humans, and
I know we bring love to all humans.

Gassing, also know as the silent gas bomb, is not the most preferred when it comes to attention techniques. Sometimes it can backfire if you just had a recent change of food. The silent gas bomb is that no-noise, eye-watering, make-people-leave-the-room fart that we can let out with little or no sound. Do not expect anyone to come right on over and pet you, but you may get let outside immediately. Another friend of mine, Trouble (how is that for a name?), used to go to the office with his human companion and sleep in a room where four or five guys were working. While sleeping, Trouble would send out silent gas bombs, each of which were good for at least three mentions of his name in the office, as well as the suggestion that he be let outside.

Bed runs are good when you have non-morning human companions. You know the type I'm talking about. They sleep in, slowly become conscious, and then take their time getting out of bed. This situation is easily remedied with a frenzy of activity. Sequoia, a mixed black lab, would start at one end of her apartment, a toy in her mouth, and run through the living room, through the office, past the bathroom, down the hall, and with a single leap from the bedroom door threshold, land on the bed, where her human was still trying to sleep. What great fun! She would promptly prance around the bed like a queen, stepping over and sometimes on her human, showing off her toy. Using this technique, Sequoia was able to train her human to get up at six a.m. every day and take her out for a walk. Then, after the walk, Sequoia could eat and relax while her human tried to sneak a few more minutes of sleep.

There are endless cute things we can do for attention because we are the kings—and queens—of cute and always ready for love and play!

Embarrassing Moments and Other Observations about Humans

All I can say is, *thank goodness I am not a poodle.* No offense, really. Some of my best friends are poodles. But I couldn't imagine being paraded outside in one of those tight little sweaters, my hair shaved into shapes meant only for bushes, and brightly colored bows tied all over my body. This isn't cute, believe me. And other dogs are laughing hard and thanking the gods above that they don't have to be subjected to this type of humiliation. We dogs don't wear clothes; this is why we are fur-covered, yet we humor our humans while they dress us up in outfits to fulfill some type of humorous or child-longing need. Humans should take that money and buy us treats and toys, in my opinion!

We all have our share of embarrassing moments and experiences we would rather forget. I will try to give you some hints on how to combat humiliation with humor.

Regarding those outfits, poodles aren't the only ones who suffer. Let's consider the holidays. Yes, that time of year when you are expected to put on stuffed reindeer antlers or a Santa hat or wear a big red bow around your neck and pose with the family for the annual card. (My poor friend Misty in Minnesota has human companions who live for those holiday cards and take pleasure in coming up with outrageous ideas. One year they harnessed him to a Santa sleigh that was pulling their one-year-old baby.)

"This is embarrassing, but sometimes we have to humor these humans."

"Who, us? Yes, we are Irish, part of the O'Greyhound clan."

The Puppies' Guide to Training Humans

125

My advice is to be a good sport. Put up with the slight humiliation and have some fun. You are loved and can indulge a little silly behavior from time to time. When you have had enough, simply roll around on the ground until the stuff comes off.

Now, there are some costumes that are to be taken seriously; these are actually uniforms that service dogs wear. These are typically orange with patches sewn on them indicating the puppy's specialty, such as seizure alert or seeing eye. These dogs have really gone beyond the basic love that all puppies give humans and are blessed with an ability to truly assist a human with his or her special needs. Seeing-eye dogs are the most common that puppies know about. They see for humans and keep them safe while walking so they do not hit or get hit by anything. This is a truly deep relationship. Other specialty puppies include search and rescue, seizure alert, physical assistance, and more. Their uniforms are worn to identify them, and they even get to go places most of us puppies do not get to go, like the post office, restaurants, private offices, and other places that prohibit just-fun puppies to accompany their humans.

Significant (Human) Others

On my list of human companion characteristics, a single guy or girl rates high. This is because there is focus. It is just the two of you. With a couple, there could be confusion over who is to feed you, walk you, and play with you. With a single guy or girl, there is no delegation of sharing the love; it is all for you. On the other hand, along with the single human companion usually comes the girlfriend or boyfriend. This is a strategic advantage for us puppies. Boyfriends and girlfriends will usually make the extra effort to get along with us puppies.

They usually realize that the rule is *love me, love my puppy,* and they will do anything to win you over. They can actually be your biggest ally and will often feed you from the table, invite you onto the couch or bed, and welcome you to come along basically anywhere.

Whatever you do, however, *do not chew their shoes.* Forget that they left them on the floor and they look like another leather chewy treat. *Never* chew their shoes! (It's amazing that Keith's girlfriend could have so many shoes and get upset over a few teething marks in one lone shoe.)

Significant others are definitely good to help you get on the furniture and for other things, such as food. Over the years I've found that significant others are effective allies. They just can't resist me when I sit at their feet and follow their hands with my big brown eyes as the food goes from plate to mouth.

I don't know how many ventriloquist stunts I've pulled by getting a significant other to speak for me. "Keith, Cochise wants some of the pasta. Can he have some bread? Do you give Cochise the leftovers?" The power of dog telepathy!

I even get Keith's guests to ask for me to join them on the sofa while watching TV. Keith normally does not let me join him on the sofa while he watches movies. This has something to do with having some remaining control over where I lie and where I do not. But when he is with a friend, he or she actually asks him for me. "Ah, Cochise wants to come up on the sofa and watch TV with us, Keith; look at him so cute." Of course, at the mention of my name, my tail commences to wag, and sometimes I have to use the sad-puppy-eye stare, but usually I get approval!

Words

Look up *dog* in the dictionary and here are some of the definitions you might find: *a worthless person, something inferior of its kind, ruin (go to the dogs), an investment not worth its price, a slow-moving or undesirable piece of merchandise, an unattractive person, a theatrical or musical flop.* This is insulting! Do the editors think we don't read?

If you would like to help eliminate the negative definitions associated with being a dog, write to *Webster's* and tell them that you, as a dog, are insulted by the negative connotations the English language has placed on being a dog. Insist that dictionaries help correct the situation by not reinforcing it through their publications. The definition of a dog should be *a carefree, intelligent, fun mammal capable of radiating unconditional love.*

Other notable words in the human language are as follows:

- Doggie bag: a way for a human to transport table scraps usually not intended for the dog

- Doggone: damn (two words—dog gone funny, isn't it?)

- Dogma: life according to dogs

- Dogged: stubbornly determined

- Dog-day afternoon: other than a great classic movie, it also describes being fully relaxed in the midday sun on your favorite piece of furniture.

- Dog-tired: how we feel after a day without our usual sixteen hours of sleep

- Dog breath: comes from eating the same food for years and not brushing our teeth

- Dog's life: what humans want to live if they did not have to work to support us

- Doggie paddle: our mode of swimming with all four legs when we do not have our lifejackets or a float to chill out on.

And let's not forget *d-o-g* spelled backward.

Then there are other words that we puppies should understand when humans use them, like Monday, Saturday, etc.

Humans have a funny way of labeling their days. One day is called Monday. This is the day they are usually tired and not in a good mood. The next day is Tuesday, followed by Wednesday, Thursday, then Friday. Friday is usually when human companions tend to relax. The day after that is Saturday. This is the day my human companion sleeps late. There is no alarm clock. There is no morning rush to leave the house, and he hangs out all day doing what he likes.

The same thing occurs the following day, which is called Sunday. Together, Saturday and Sunday are called the weekend. This is important for us dogs to remember because human companions act differently based upon the day. Ah, dog life. For us, every day is like their Saturday.

I have tried to get my human companion to treat every day like Saturday, but it has not worked. (Even I do not have all the answers to human training.) My observation is that it takes many dog lives to get a human to understand that every day is Saturday. But by then they are not as active as they used to be in their younger days. In fact, the funny thing is that humans call this time *being retired.* If we look at this word, it means *re-tired,* or *tired again.* Then finally, every day *is* Saturday, and they are tired again. What fun is that?

This is one area I believe warrants more research: how to help humans understand that every day is absolutely the same. To treat every day as if it were Saturday (except for those of us who worship the big dog on Saturdays, in which case maybe Sunday is a better analogy). But basically to enjoy fully each day, take naps, play, take a walk, cuddle, take another nap, and play more.

Pet Peeves

First, for those puppy readers that are not familiar with the term *pet peeve*, I will provide some vocabulary history for your understanding. Who knows, one day you may be on a game show like *Puppy Jeopardy!* or *Woof or Consequences* and will recall this tidbit of knowledge to win squeaky toys for life.

Peeve means something that is particularly annoying; it is a relatively new word. It was first printed in approximately 1911 and is derived from *peevish*, a fourteenth-century word meaning *ill-tempered.* The combined term *pet peeve* means a very personal irritant and first appeared around

1919. So by deduction, the term *pet* in this case means *very personal*. Of course, we are talking about the dark ages of puppy history, when we were still largely treated as hunting companions or work companions (herding, etc.). But even then, in the dark ages of puppy history, the human was beginning to relate to us in a personal manner. Of course, the term *pet* does not provide an absolute correlation to puppies. To be fair, there are other pets—horses, cats, fish, snakes, lizards. But to be as objective as I can be, puppies are the most personal of all of these with humans in today's modern age. Maybe kittens could be considered…nah. Just look at history. Wild dog or wolf puppies were the humans' first pets in the prehistoric era. That is a human term I never understood. How can any thing be *pre* history? Isn't that the definition of history, what happened before?

There I go once again. Keith has so much fun typing and keeping up with my thought tangents…Oops, there is another one; back to the topic. Pet peeves, things that humans do that annoy puppies.

Number One: Not washing our food and water bowl before each meal.

Why don't humans wash our food bowls or plates after every meal? Keith would never eat two meals on the same plate without washing it before each meal. He even has a robot thing that does it for him, called a dishwasher. When he opens the dishwasher door, steam comes out, meaning Keith's plates, etc., have even been rinsed, washed, rinsed again, and then sterilized. Why doesn't he put my bowls through the same process?

I discussed this with Keith one day, and he was shocked at the simplicity and logic in my request. He had never thought about it. Of course, he would wash my bowls out periodically; he is not a complete tyrant. As soon as I brought up the comparison of how he treats his bowl and how he treats my bowl, he apologized profusely. He then went out and bought me three new bowls.

Keith was so thoughtful that he got me three different bowls; each has a different design or saying. This way I get a clean bowl for each meal, and I can be sure by the change in design. The variety of bowls also makes my meals a little more entertaining. This may not sound like such a great point, but eating every meal from the same green bowl for a few years is boring, and a changeup is greatly appreciated.

One thing I really like about what Keith did is that the three bowls are not only different in design but are also different materials. One is a shiny metal bowl, one is a plastic bowl, and one (my favorite) is ceramic. I know you puppies are wondering why my favorite is the ceramic bowl. Well, it is because it is the same kind of bowl Keith uses. He and I actually have a matching set. So he eats out of the same kind of bowl as I do; that is love. I have never seen a human eating out of a metal bowl. I have only rarely seen humans eat out of a plastic bowl, usually when they are camping or on a boat or someplace they are concerned about weight and breakage.

Of course, the pet industry creates a whole product line of bowls that are bottom heavy or have non-skid bottoms, and of course, they are large diameter and low profile. But we don't need a special bowl; we just want a clean bowl.

To help with the problem of a moving bowl while drinking or eating, Keith simply put the bowls on a non-skid mat. Humans call them placemats and have one for every person at their table. So not only do I have a change of bowls, but I have different mats to eat on also. Is this too much to ask for from your human?

Now with all this insight, here is a technique to train your human on this pet peeve. It is not 100 percent effective, but I suggest you might leave your copy of this book open to this chapter somewhere your human will find it. In addition to that, try licking your bowl when you are finished eating. Humans usually interpret this as either we are still hungry or loved the meal so much we have to get every last drop. However, they actually will say to you, "Are you licking your bowl clean?" *Yes, clean!* They actually use the term but do not think of it literally. Your message back to them should be, "Yes, I have to *lick* it clean, but it would be nice to have a variety of bowls that are properly washed between meals."

There is one technique that can be used in extreme cases. Serge, a chocolate lab friend of mine, had the same bowl for more than three years. This is just inhumane. Serge figures that during those three years his bowls were washed about twenty times (once every few months!). So one day he simply ate his bowl! Yes, that is right, Serge ate his bowl. It was plastic, thank goodness. He claimed that after so many years, the bowl smelled and tasted like food. Years of absorption had caused his bowl to taste like food. Now, this is an extreme technique to get your human to change your bowl. I use it as an example only and do not endorse other puppies eating their bowls.

A slightly more reasonable approach, and one that has been tried and proven, is to simply chew a side or the edge of the bowl, making it somewhat unattractive. Humans will not want that unattractive bowl lying around, so they will change it for a new one.

So there you go. Your human companion would never eat two meals on the same plate or bowl, and you should not either. Let's move on to my next pet peeve.

Number Two: Last names.

We are part of the family, so we should have the family name. I was walking with Keith through a pet cemetery a few weeks ago in southern California, Huntington Beach area, I think. At first, I thought it was a bit creepy to just walk around a cemetery where you do not know anyone. But as we walked around, I realized how great a place it was. Humans had arranged pictures, squeaky toys, and other memorable items around the headstone of their dearly beloved that had passed away to puppy or kitten heaven.

One of the things I came to realize was that some only had their first names on the stones. This seemed somewhere between anonymous and lost. I have been to some human cemeteries. The last one was with a dear friend of Keith's, who visited her father's grave every Christmas Day, which was the day he passed. I noticed that there were first and last names on every human headstone. In some cases, more names, such as middle names and nicknames. There was not one headstone that just said, *In memory of Thomas* or *Julie.* Even humans whose names are not known have two names— they are called Jane Doe and John Doe. So when I walked through the pet cemetery, I was impressed by the ones that did have last names. How great a way to be related! It is like family! Leaving off our last name is not really the fault of the human; this is a simple oversight because we do not require the formal paperwork that human puppies do, like birth certificates, where they have to place a first and last name. Usually the veterinarians will place our humans' last names on our files, and that is as far as it goes. This is just another area we puppies have to help our humans understand. At times I think we might be angels for these humans.

One technique to help our humans is, during our first few months with them, they can introduce us by our first and last name. Visitors comment, "Oh, this is your new puppy? How cute!"

And the human can say, "Yes, this is Cochise Barksdale, our new member of the family." This makes it clear that we are a part of the family.

Our last name should also be used on headstones and those name charms on our necklaces, or as humans call them, the nametags on our collars. And of course, if you publish a book, you should have your last name printed. I had to discuss this with my publisher because they also wanted a social security number for tax reporting. "Tax reporting," I said to them. "I'm a dog. We are exempt." They just thought that because I was published with my first and last name, the system would try and track me down as a human. Good luck finding Fido Bonaparte.

Number Three: Dog Tags, Chips, and Tattoos.

These are evolutionary identification methods for us puppies. They are all good things, and I fully endorse every puppy to have one or two ways to be identified, should you get lost for any reason. The only item I have here as my pet peeve is first, include our family name, and do not use the words *belongs to*. We are not property; we are not a lost suitcase that the airline is trying to identify. We are a member of the family. So leave the *belongs to* off. Use *If lost, please call,* or *My human companion is...*

Number Four: Jewelry.

When Keith wears a neck chain and goes to bed, he takes it off. His girlfriend would do the same; they never sleep in their jewelry. So why should I? This necklace he put on me never comes off. Day, night, rain, shine, beach, woods—I am always wearing the thing. I have worn it so much that it has permanently created a wave in my hair around the neck. So I have two points about this pet peeve. First, ask your human to take it off you when you are home or going to sleep. It is much more comfortable to sleep without it. We need to wear it occasionally when we are put on the leash for a walk or when company comes over, to look dressed up. The rest of the time, leave it in the drawer.

Second point: buy me several styles and colors. I like an assortment. Keith has several styles he wears. I had only four until I was five years old. The only reason they changed is that I outgrew the first two and ate the third. (It was leather; couldn't tell it apart from my rawhide. Same claim on that girl's red shoe, by the way.)

So one day Keith came home with five different collars. (I prefer the term *neck straps* or *necklace*.) Yep, five different ones. Seems about this time that pet boutiques started catching up with the thought that we had style and taste and demanded more from the fashion world. I got a shiny black one, a cool burgundy and green cloth one, one with spikes for my punk nights, a reflective one for those nights at the dog disco, and a camouflage one for hunting. *Hunting?* I don't hunt; well, it seems that camouflage has become a cool thing to wear anywhere. We live in the city. I would think the camouflage here should have had a brick or asphalt-and-gum pattern to match my surroundings.

NUMBER FIVE: DOG BEDS.

Simply, this pet peeve is that it is nice to have our own round fleece bed filled with cedar chips and all, but we want to sit and sleep with our human. So no need for these special beds; really, our human's bed is our bed. I know not all of you agree. Humans can be difficult to sleep with. They toss and turn around. They get up and go the bathroom in the middle of the night. They snore or talk in their sleep. So I can understand that sometimes you just want a good night's sleep and to leave your human alone on his or her own bed. But there is no better bonding time than bed cuddling.

So if you are not in your human's bed because you choose to sleep elsewhere, there are sofas, chairs, and carpets, other places that are quite nice and cozy. The dog bed, I find, is just a good place to put my toys, store some food nuggets, keep a nice odor of me around the home. *Sniff, sniff, lick, lick!*

Learning and Lessons

I found in life that a lesson provides us the knowledge to ask further questions. This is continual learning. An answer to a question generates another question. So what I have attempted to organize in this book is a beginning.

The relationship we have with our human companions is a dear one. While we train them to adapt to living with us, they also bring us great companionship. They watch over us, love us, play with us, and bond emotionally with us.

Humans tend to live longer than the average

dog life. When we leave them, we want to leave them with a feeling of love, appreciation, and the desire to have another dog companion. We know the next companion is not a comparison to us or a replacement but a continuation of the unconditional love in their life. And you know the next dog companion will appreciate *your* training when he or she is automatically placed next to the bed in a box as a puppy, given the free run of the yard, or held while napping. *Sniff, sniff, lick, lick, cuddle!* Unconditional love is all we need.

It is thus with these first writings that I hope to have helped puppies achieve this goal with their human companions. I view this work not as an end product but as a continual development toward universal unconditional love. Just as this book was going into its second edition, I noted training advances such as puppy strollers, puppy carrier bags in designer styles, and more puppies on planes going on vacations with their humans. These are major trends that are evolving. Let's all apaws the good humans, pawsome work! Sniff sniff, lick lick!

Simple Dog Wisdom to Live By

- Nap daily.
- Play daily.
- Nap again daily.
- Do the happy dance when you are happy.
- Be consistent, and you will get what you want.
- Licks are better than barks.
- Treat every day like Saturday.
- Remember who feeds you.

- Don't settle for original flavor.

- Spread as much fun and love as possible, without borders or conditions.

Now let's not forget our prayers: May the great dog in the sky watch over all of us and our human companions and show us all the way to unconditional love.

Cochise Barksdale

Play daily!

Have a cute or funny story or photograph about your human and puppy companionship?

Send it to Cochise Barksdale at:

cochise@puppysguide.com.

Visit our Web site at

www.puppysguide.com.